The Honeymoon Is Over

**Other Close to Home Books
by John McPherson**

Close to Home
One Step Closer to Home
Dangerously Close to Home
Home: The Final Frontier

Treasury Collection

Close to Home Revisited

Also from John McPherson

High School Isn't Pretty
Close to Home: A Book of Postcards

The Honeymoon Is Over

By John McPherson

ZondervanPublishingHouse

Grand Rapids, Michigan

A Division of HarperCollins *Publishers*

ISBN: 0-310-21399-1

For Rowena and Jim

The Puzney High Wombats are undefeated
since they got their new uniforms.

The Wilsons and the Fegleys quickly regretted
paying 20 bucks extra for a room with a view.

"Oh, wait! I think I found the problem!
I've been using the Nebraska map instead
of the Vermont map!"

Having just learned that she won the lottery,
hair stylist Ramona Yotz has a little fun with the one
customer who failed to tip her in 12 years.

Vera ignores the first rule of grocery shopping:
Never shop when you're hungry.

With a typical wedding cake costing $300,
Ed and Linda opted for the more
economical wedding pizza.

Bamford County was notorious for its speed traps.

"Poor Muffin! What a nasty hairball that was!"

"Because, Mr. Westcott, your insurance doesn't cover the cost of a hospital room after gall bladder surgery."

After the slide projector broke, Dave's presentation to the board of directors took a drastic turn for the worse.

Functional as well as elegant, No-pest earrings
are becoming quite the rage.

"Hey, kid. I'll give you five bucks
if you'll crawl around in there, find a little boy
with a red-striped shirt and bring him out."

14

Kevin finally found a way to keep his
head down when he swings.

"Let me know if you find a set of dentures
in there, ma'am."

Somehow, the big drug-store chains just don't instill the same feeling of confidence that one gets from a neighborhood drug store.

After the seventh consecutive viewing of
"Barney Goes to Cleveland," Alan suffers
a spontaneous boredom attack.

More and more students are turning to
private coaching firms to help them
score higher on the SAT.

"While you're at it, get me a cheeseburger,
a large order of fries, and chocolate shake."

"Will you stop kidding yourself?! You are *not* getting any exercise!"

22

"I'm sorry, ma'am, but I'm afraid your husband doesn't qualify as a carry-on-item."

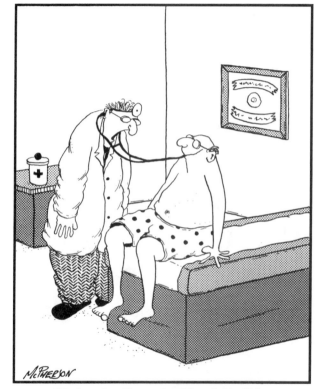

"Mr. Farnsley, I haven't got the slightest idea what song you're humming. Please take the stethoscope out of your mouth so we can finish your examination."

Deep down inside, Coach Knott had always wanted to be a math teacher.

Thanks to Muffin, Karl hadn't had to shampoo his hair in 2½ years.

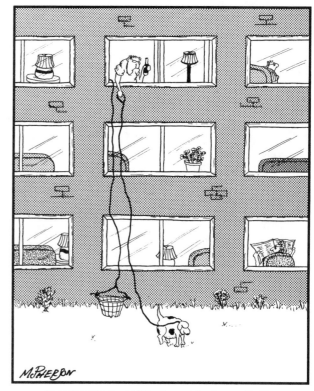

Larry had been getting increasingly apathetic about walking the dog.

It wasn't long before students started to take advantage of
Mrs. Grindle's nearsightedness.

Desperate people do desperate things.

Gary was beginning to have some concerns
about his new group health plan.

The trend in the '90s is toward
highly specialized colleges.

"Yep, here it is right here. Your extended
warranty covers only the glove compartment,
dome light and vanity mirror."

"I am not *wearing* stockings, thank you!"

"All right! All right! You've made your point, Dad!
I'll get rid of my earring, I swear!"

"And what seems to be the problem with the shampoo, ma'am?"

Catering to customers who frequent drive-through restaurants, some car manufacturers are installing driver's side burger clips.

Dan just wasn't working out as a spotter
for the gynmastics team.

Management at the Zebco Novelty Co.
continued to be puzzled by the company's
declining productivity.

"And . . . uh . . . how about your . . . uh . . . sideburns?
Do you want them trimmed, too?"

After hearing that electric blankets emit harmful
electromagnetic waves, Norm and Sheila
switched to a wood-fired blanket.

"He's half black Lab and half Siberian husky."

"Who would've thought that a car this size
could fit underneath a tractor trailer?!"

Company chairman Lloyd Fegman didn't have much patience
for what he considered to be dumb questions.

"For heaven's sake! If it's that big a deal to you, let's get cable!"

In recent years, many companies have found it necessary to employ Game Police.

The Home Shopping Network expands its product line.

"Could you go over the part about the
seat belts one more time?"

Murphy's Law of New Shirts: No matter how many pins you remove from a new shirt, there's always one more.

"Frank, Doug Parsons wants to know if you can help put up Christmas lights on the big spruce tree in their front yard."

"I don't *care* if you're sentimental! We need a new mattress!"

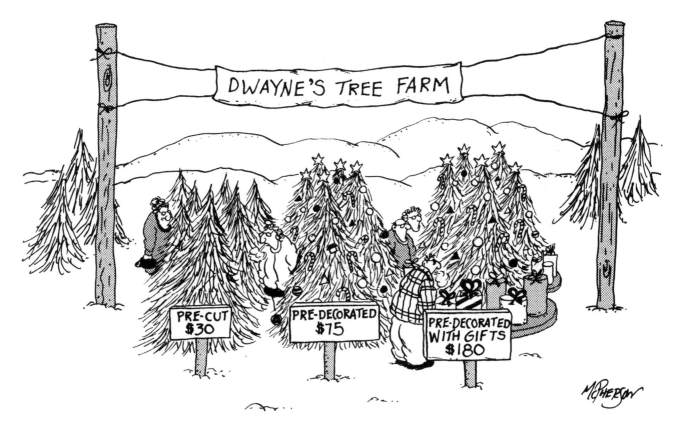

As soon as Mrs. Felster began to read the minutes of the last meeting, the board members knew she was not going to work out as the new secretary.

Virgil's new litterbox-emptying device
worked great until his neighbors down in 4B
returned from their three-week vacation.

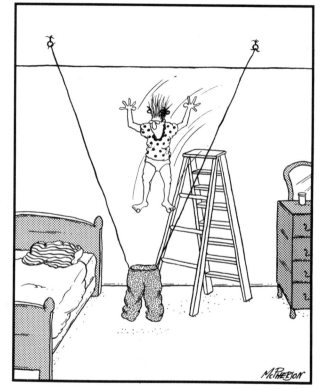

Clarice was having a difficult time accepting
the fact that she was no longer a size 8.

To prevent family members from monopolizing the shower, the Fegleys wisely had the faucet handles installed outside the bathroom.

"Take the entire bottle of pills immediately!"

Attempts to make the church newsletter
more exciting were getting out of hand.

"I don't think you understand! I said, the pacifier fell out somewhere back in the airport! Tell the pilot to turn the plane around — now!"

Jerry could almost taste the sale.

"I accidentally dropped my gum into the money canister. Would you mind returning it with my cash?"

Thanks to her new blanket security system, Mary Ann was able to thwart Jim's attempts to steal the blanket.

Mrs. Lasky hoped that oral midterms in Spanish 201 would give students a unique cultural experience.

No one could guess gifts like Jean Morrissey.

By tattooing employees each time they take a sick day,
Feckley Industries has been able to dramatically reduce sick leave abuse.

"I'm sick of stubbing my toe on this doorway."

"Good news! The exploratory surgery
turned up negative!"

It didn't take much to upset Mrs. Stegler.

"Oh, *LASER*. Well, I'm sorry, but that still looks like an 'O' on your application to me."

At the Hair Club for Men quality-control center.

"It's one of the new easy-open twist-off caps."

Aunt Ruth had a knack for getting children gifts
that their parents hated.

The Lampleys discovered a simple way to pass
the food during Christmas dinner.

Lyle liked to think of himself as a full-service waiter.

Although she had endured many horrendous gas-station rest rooms, Susan had a feeling that this one would go down in infamy.

"Ever since we had the grease fire in the kitchen,
George has been a bit overprotective."

"Good afternoon, sir. My name is Daryl,
and I'll be your ticketing officer."

Rather than risk biting into a chocolate that
she didn't like, Barb pulled out her
creme-filling detector.

"Let's put it on high for 20 minutes.
She's gotta fall asleep after that."

"Well, Brad, now that we both agree you deserve a raise,
what do you say we make things interesting?"

"It's all yours!"

Just minutes into their shopping spree,
Jean and Lisa are ambushed by a gang
of hostile cosmetic clerks.

"Oh, those are our wedding photos. We had them all taken using that new 3-D technology!"

"Your root canal is pretty straightforward, Mrs. Zagler, so I'm going to turn things over to the Auto-Dentist. If you have any problems, just pull on that cord above your head."

"It's Stephen King's latest book in extra-large type."

The Wickman family did its best to make the usually dull task of detrimming the tree more lively.

Vern was beginning to have some doubts
about the builder he had selected.

"The salesman said this is a state-of-the-art model
that doesn't need a remote."

Although no one could quite put a finger on it,
there was something strangely unnerving
about the new biology teacher.

"Could I please have six or seven
extra air-sickness bags?"

Having spotted some acquaintances,
Vera activates the instant grandchildren-photo
display on her purse.

"Does this sweater make me look bulky?"

"This new attachment I got makes ironing shirts a piece of cake."

"Be sure to take these with plenty of water."

**Play-Doh and Toro team up to take snowblower
technology to a whole new level.**

"It only takes Susan B. Anthony dollars!"

The guys down at Zeffler's Garage were having hours of fun with the remote-control squeal device they had hidden in Mrs. Lambert's car.

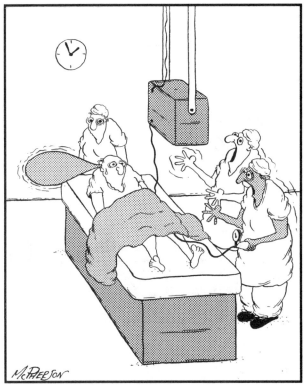

Ted's balloon angioplasty procedure gets off to a rough start.

"I think the satellite dish just blew off the roof."

"How about you, sir: Would you like the house wine also?"

"Now *this* is what I call an ice storm!"

Andy's dispute with the jerk in 4C heats up.

"Our sneeze guard is out for repairs.
Would you mind wearing this helmet?"

"Remind me never to ask the youth group
to help fold the church bulletins again."

"I was under the impression that it was the *restaurant* that revolved."

"How on earth could I have known that your coat
was caught on the door handle?"

"The plumber says that the replacement parts for the toilet won't be in for three more weeks, and he left us this."

"This isn't our house, you idiot!"

The Sunday Bugle Herald adapts a popular children's book
feature and introduces pop-up personal ads.

"Will you quit whining?! You're the one who wanted
real maple syrup."

"For 25 bucks I'll shovel a path to your snow blower."

"I got sick of cleaning up hairballs."

"Oh, my! This is *much* worse than I thought! I'm afraid we may have to pull *all* of these lower teeth! Take a look and see if you agree, Ms. Comstock."

"I rigged up the phone so you can talk while you're cooking."

"Two more records to go and I'll have logged every single item we own for our insurance records."

"Whoa! Hold up. I think we goofed.
She's in for an appendectomy."

Comet Airlines revolutionizes the airline industry
by offering ultra-super-duper first class.

The personnel department at Carner Industries
was known for its impersonal interviewing process.

"It can be very dangerous to suppress a hiccup."

"Wait, don't call the plumber yet.
I think I can see the end of the plunger!"

After four hours of lugging a 28-pound toddler
around a mall, Doug is stricken by a case of
Baby-Backpack Syndrome.

"I need to use the rest room. Hang on to this end of the rope so I can find my way back."

Hoping to bolster its sagging ticket sales, Comet Airlines introduces its new line of glass-bottomed jets.

"Do you want to be the one to go outside when it's minus-15 to get some firewood? All right then, quit complaining!"

It was several weeks before the
Millsville Department of Public Works
realized that it had mistakenly purchased
a Zamboni rather than a street cleaner.

Bruce activates the new telemarketer-zap
feature on his phone.

"We finally got smart and had
speed bumps installed."

"Well, we found out what was
causing that squealing noise. Your wife
had been sitting on a tack."

The staff at Wilmont Obstetrics just couldn't resist
pulling the fake sonogram trick.

"It's a merry-go-round for kids who don't get to spend enough time with their dads."

"Will you stop whining? I told you three times that this restaurant requires men to wear a jacket and tie!"

Many felt that the company's new dress code
was too stringent.

"For the third time, sir, there are *no* other seats available! Now please take your seat."

"You let that cavity go far too long."

Another priceless camcorder moment is destroyed by a loudmouthed stranger.

"Those morons downstairs got their kid a model rocket kit."

"Unfortunately, Mr. Mendrick,
your insurance doesn't cover some
of the more conventional hearing aids."

"They say if we switch back now, we'll get 25
percent off all calls made to people with red hair."

The Candle Glow Inn introduces its new scratch-and-sniff menus.

"So far we've been able to heat the entire house using nothing but junk mail."

"But that's the beauty of it, Rita! I don't have to worry about my fat intake today. I'm having a quadruple bypass tomorrow!"

"What kind of an idiot hires two seventh-graders to install vinyl siding?!"

In a cruel twist of fate, the Bowmans discover that they live
between the Publishers Clearing House Grand Prize and First Prize winners.

"Excuse me, folks, can we squeeze by?"

108

In an incredible stroke of luck, Brian discovers that the Final Jeopardy question is the same as the 20-point bonus question on his take-home midterm.

Take Your Child to Work Day at Fernview Hospital.

"The actual parts for your exhaust system weren't available, but we were able to modify some parts we had in stock."

Wayne chooses an inappropriate moment to pull the old "severed-finger-in-a-box" gag.

The latest in family health care:
infection detectors.

As a convenience to their married customers, some grocery stores have installed cellular phones on their shopping carts.

Talking scales: Proof that technology
isn't always good.

"All I need to do is give that cord one good, solid yank and all of the toys are instantly picked up."

In a dramatic sting operation, FBI agents crack down on restaurant employees who don't wash their hands after using the rest room.

"It's your turn to empty the litter box."

"We're not sure what this thing is, but we took it out and your car seems to be running a lot smoother."

The First Law of Air Travel: The distance to your connecting gate is directly proportional to the amount of luggage you are carrying and inversely proportional to the amount of time you have.

119

The latest technology in the quest
for faster pizza delivery.

Don and Ellen Finley attempt to leave their
four-month-old with a sitter for the first time.

Knowing that there was always bumper-to-bumper traffic at this spot during rush hour, Pete and Chuck established a lucrative partnership.

For the sake of convenience, parents with several children are opting to have in-home pharmacists.

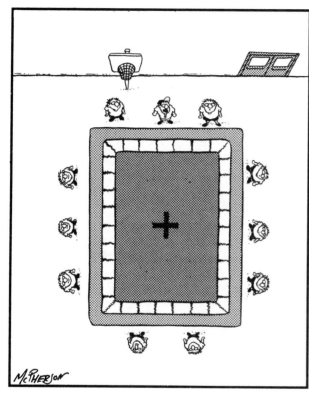

"Let go of the ceiling, Wilkins!"

"I never heard of someone having salmon as pets."

Roger would go to any lengths to land this account.

When dieting goes too far.

"Since when did they start
alphabetizing grocery stores?"

"Relax, I know what I'm doing."

After a series of poor performance reviews,
Bob was given a pink slip.

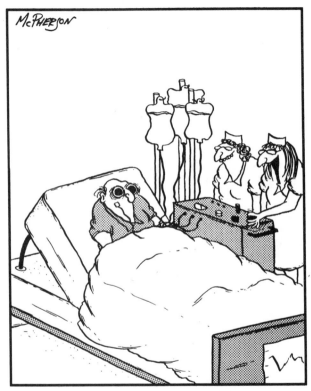

"Hey, Carol! Look how big his eyes get when you turn this blue dial *way* up!"

"It's a reminder from our dentist that your six-month checkup is next Wednesday at 2 o'clock."